Mothers and Daughters Are Connected by the Heart

ISBN: 978-1-68088-214-8

◪ and Blue Mountain Press are registered in U.S. Patent and Trademark Office. Certain trademarks are used under license.

Printed in China.
Second Printing: 2018

⊕ This book is printed on recycled paper.

This book is printed on paper that has been specially produced to be acid free (neutral pH) and contains no groundwood or unbleached pulp. It conforms with the requirements of the American National Standards Institute, Inc., so as to ensure that this book will last and be enjoyed by future generations.

Blue Mountain Arts, Inc.
P.O. Box 4549, Boulder, Colorado 80306

Mothers and Daughters Are *Connected* by the Heart

Written and Illustrated by
Heather Stillufsen

Blue Mountain Press™
Boulder, Colorado

Mothers and *daughters*
fill each other's lives
with never-ending
love

A *daughter* is
a mother's *treasure*

♥

A *mother* is
a daughter's first *friend*

It's the *little moments*
mothers and daughters
share that make life
beautiful

Like *mother,*
like *daughter*

A *daughter* is...

- ♥ life's greatest gift
- ♥ a hand to hold
- ♥ a heart to love
- ♥ a friend for life
- ♥ pure joy
- ♥ someone to laugh with
- ♥ someone to cry with
- ♥ someone to remember with
- ♥ a dream come true

A mother...

- gives with all her heart
- loves without limits
- is a best friend, a teacher, and a great listener
- helps you find the rainbow on a rainy day
- will never judge you
- always puts her daughter's happiness ahead of her own

Mothers and daughters
take *time* to
gather *memories*
together

Mothers and daughters
are *always* there
for each other,
come rain or *shine*

Mothers and *daughters*
don't have to
see eye to eye
to feel *heart* to *heart*

Sometimes,
just spending time
together
is all the therapy
needed

To a *daughter,*
a mother will always be
someone to look up to

♥

To a *mother,*
a daughter will always
be her little girl

Mothers and daughters
have a *special* bond
that lasts *forever*

Mothers *make* the
hard times *easier*

Daughters *make* the
good times *better*

Mothers and daughters
share one of the
best gifts in life:
to love and be loved
unconditionally

Mothers and *daughters* are…

- ♥ coffee buddies
- ♥ secret keepers
- ♥ therapists
- ♥ travel partners
- ♥ confidantes
- ♥ best friends for life

It's not *what* we have in
our lives, but *who*
we have in our lives
that matters

Side by side
or miles apart,
mothers and *daughters*
will always be
connected by the
heart

About the Author

Heather Stillufsen fell in love with drawing as a child and has been holding a pencil ever since. She is best known for her delicate and whimsical illustration style, which has become instantly recognizable. From friendship to family to fashion, Heather's art

Photo by Christine E. Allen

demonstrates a contemporary sensibility for people of all ages. Her words are written from the heart and offer those who read them the hope of a brighter day and inspiration to live life to the fullest.

In addition to her line of greeting cards, Heather's refreshing and elegant illustrations can be found on calendars, journals, cards, art prints, hand-painted needlepoint canvases, and more.

She currently lives in New Jersey with her husband, two daughters, and chocolate Lab.